Praise for Gerry the Giraffe:

"It is no secret that I am a major fan of giraffes and *Gerry the Giraffe* [...] harder than ever to be a kid growing up these days. *Gerry the Giraffe* [...] trying your best and hanging in there when things get tough. The illu[...] wonderfully loose, playful, and beautiful moving pieces of art that kee[...] both the eyes and the heart. A fabulous read for parents and kids alik[...]"

J.H. Everett, Author/Illustrator, *Haunted Histories*

"I love the illustrations. The colors are cheerful and eye catching. The story teaches perseverance, as Gerry wakes up early each morning to practice and train. This book is just the right length to hold a child's attention without taxing their attention span."

Anne B, 5 Star Review, *Readers Favorite*

"*Gerry The Giraffe* is a fun, original story about a sports minded giraffe who loves to play volleyball. After Gerry isn't asked to join the team, or even invited to summer volleyball camp, he questions what he can do to improve his game. This story touches on themes of not giving up and overcoming life's challenges. It is sure to inspire young readers to realize that through practice and hard work they can accomplish their goals just like *Gerry the Giraffe* does."

Merrily Kutner, Author of *Down on the Farm*.

"*Gerry the Giraffe* is a story you will want to have your children hear again and again. Gerry is the smallest volleyball playing giraffe in his village. When all his friends go off to volleyball camp without him, he has to deal with disappointment and heartache. The message in this story is one of perseverance and hard work, something kids benefit from hearing in the context of stories. The illustrations are unique and will inspire many drawings in your home. At the end of the app there are fact pages and a parents "reading strategy" page with tips for making the reading more meaningful. Enjoy learning from Gerry that hard work and persistence not only can have external rewards, but provides internal joy too."

Carolina Nugent, Director of Education, *KinderTown*

"Along with its easily relatable situations appropriate for all ages, *Gerry the Giraffe* is also chock full of fantastic art and animations. Readers will squeal with delight as they find hidden messages and quirky phrases scattered among the illustrations. In artist Jennifer Mercede's signature style, bold marks and color-filled pages exude a cozy familiarity for children while wowing parents with their elegance and layered qualities."

Beth Demmon, Editor, *Oopsy daisy*

"Gerry is an adorable character that kids will identify with, as he struggles to become the best at something he loves through practice and perseverance. Parents and educators will appreciate the underlying messages about sticking to a goal and making the most of your strengths in this colorful and touching tale."

Carisa Kluver, Co-Founder, *Digital-Storytime.com*

"This is a great story about teaching your children how to set goals and follow through with them."

Alison Hirst, *The iMums*

Text © 2012 by Melissa Northway
Illustrations © 2012 by Jennifer Mercede
All rights reserved

Typeset in Avant Garde
Manufactured in the United States of America
ISBN – 13: 978-0-9883086-0-2
ISBN – 10: 0988308606

Polka Dots Publishing
4521 Campus Drive #360
Irvine, CA 92612
mcube@sbcglobal.net

For more fun and games visit:
www.melissanorthway.com

Gerry the Giraffe

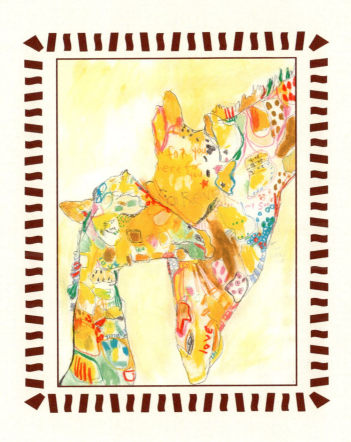

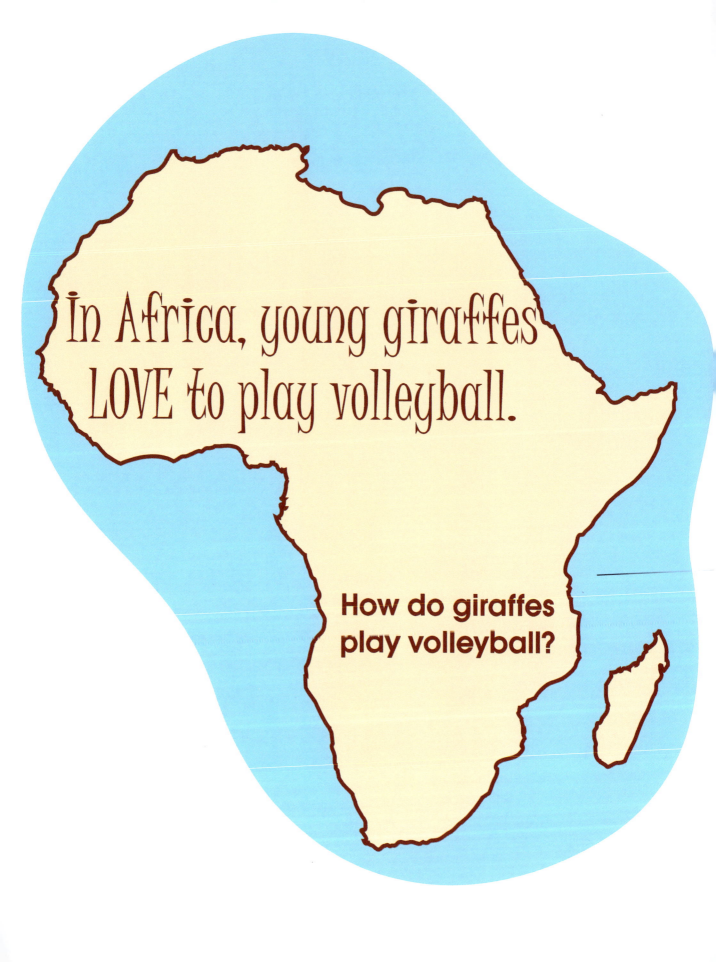

They bump and set and spike the ball with their heads and necks.

Gerry the Giraffe played the game any chance he could get.

One summer day, the entire giraffe "Super Sonics" team went to volleyball camp . . . except Gerry.

"What's wrong, Gerry?" his mother asked.
Gerry stared down at the ground.
"Mom, no one wants me on the team because I'm small and they think I can't play.

I didn't even get invited to volleyball camp!"
He plopped down on the ground.

His mother smiled. "Well, you're young and you'll grow in time. But is there anything you can do right now to become a better player?"
"I'm not sure; I need to think about that."

He wandered to his favorite shady tree.
He thought and thought and thought.
How could he become a better player?

Suddenly, he had an idea. He couldn't get taller right now, but if he practiced really hard, he could become the best volleyball player he could be. As Dad always said, "Keep trying – don't give up."

He galloped home with a goofy grin on his face

"Mom, Mom . . . I know what I can do!"

"I see you're all excited," his mother exclaimed.

Gerry's eyes widened. "I am going to practice every day, work really hard, and eat as many Acacia leaves as possible," he said.

"Then I'll get as strong as a rhinoceros and as agile as a gazelle!"

His mother grinned and felt his muscles.
He started putting on his workout clothes.
"I'll even stop eating so many
'super duper' berry bursts."

That summer, Gerry woke up early every morning.
He ran and ran and ran.

Some days it was hard getting up so early.
He just wanted to pull the blanket over his head
and go back to sleep.

But to be his best, he had to work hard.

He bounced the volleyball on his head up and down for hours.

He jumped over rocks, tree stumps, and other animals.

He loved jumping over Tom Tortoise,
though Tom didn't seem to even notice.

"Come on. Let's race!"
Gerry yelled to Lenny Lion and Zoe Zebra.
He zipped by them and
raced the cheetahs at the water hole.

But he couldn't beat the cheetahs
– they were so fast!
"I'll never be as fast as they are," he thought.

Although he couldn't beat the cheetahs,
he felt stronger and stronger every day.

Then one day, he saw the cheetahs on their way to the water hole.
Pouring on the speed, he ran and called, "Catch me if you can, cheetahs!"

It was a close race but…
Gerry beat the cheetahs to the water hole!
"No fair." the cheetahs shouted.
"We weren't ready!"

By summer's end, Gerry grew and grew and grew.

He was taller than most of the Acacia trees,

and EVEN taller than his mom and dad!

When the other giraffes returned from camp,
he was taller than all of them, too.

"Wow! You can almost touch the clouds, Gerry,"
the other giraffes remarked.
"You are acing every serve!" they said.

Gerry spiked another ball over the net.
"I worked hard all summer."

"We want you on our team!" said the captain.
"Yeah!" everyone shouted.
Gerry nodded.

Now, when Gerry isn't leading his team to victory, he is teaching young giraffes his favorite moves.

Fun Facts About Giraffes

Giraffes can live up to 25 years.

The thorny leaves of an Acai tree are a giraffe's favorite meal.

Giraffes have excellent vision, which enables them to spot predators from far away.

Other animals, such as zebras and antelopes, like to stay close to giraffes because giraffes can warn them of predators.

Each giraffe has a pattern that is unique.

This pattern helps giraffes blend into their environment and protects them from predators, such as lions.

Giraffes are known for their long necks, which have seven vertebrae – the same number as humans and most all other mammals have.

Giraffes' long necks and tongues (which can reach 18 inches) allow them to eat leaves from tall branches.

Giraffes spend about half the day foraging for leaves and buds on trees and shrubs.

A giraffe's heart beats up to 170 times per minute – twice the rate of humans. This allows the blood flow to reach its head, which is two meters away from its heart.

Adult giraffes use their bowl-shaped hooves to protect themselves and their young.

Sources:

www.philadelphiazoo.com

http://kids.nationalgeographic.com

www.giraffeconservation.org

Photographs courtesy of:
Bruce Wayne Carter
www.brucewaynephoto.com

You can adopt a giraffe through the World Wildlife Organization (WWF) at: www.worldwildlife.org

Fun Facts About Africa

Africa is the second-largest of the Earth's seven continents and it makes up approximately 22% of the Earth's total land area.

Nearly one billion people live in Africa. The general population in many African countries is young, and more than half of the people are under the age of 25.

Africa makes up approximately 16% of the world's population.

Nigeria is the most populated country in Africa, with an estimated population of 135 million people, and Egypt is second, with more than 76 million people.

Four of the five fastest land animals that live in Africa are the cheetah, the wildebeest, the lion, and the Thomson's gazelle. They can all run more than 50 miles per hour; the cheetah reaches speeds greater than 70 miles per hour.

The African elephant is the world's largest living land animal. The male of the species weighs up to 6.5 tons.

With over 170 million speakers, Arabic is the most common language. The African continent is home to over 2,000 languages.

Experts estimate that there are at least 3,000 distinct ethnic tribes in Africa.

Sudan is the largest country in Africa, with a total area of 2.5 million square kilometers. The smallest country is the island nation of The Seychelles, with an area of 453 square kilometers.

Soccer (called football) and cricket are the two most popular sports in Africa. Both sports were introduced during colonial times, and African teams have enjoyed great international success.

South Africa occupies only about 1% of the Earth's land surface but is home to almost 10% of the world's bird, fish and plant species and about 6% of its mammal and reptile species.

Photographs courtesy of Bruce Wayne Carter

References:

Bowden, Rob. 2005. Africa. Strongsville, OH: Gareth Stevens Publishing.

Gates, Henry Louis Jr. 1999. Wonders of the African World. New York, NY: Routledge.

Habeeb, William Mark & Robert I. Rotberg. 2004. Africa: Facts and Figures. Broomall, PA: Mason Crest.

Reader, John. 1999. Africa: A Biography of the Continent. New York, NY: Knopf Publishing Group.

www.kids.nationalgeographic.com.

Smarty Activity Reading Strategies

This is a product of Cyndie Sebourn and Sascyn Publishing, Inc.

APP: *Gerry the Giraffe*
Activity Title: Reading Strategies
Approximate Grade Level: 1-3
Subject(s): Language Arts: Reading Strategies/Literacy in Geography and Science

Discussion Questions with Deeper Thinking

The following are Reading Strategies/Discussion Questions that are designed by a National Board Certified Teacher and are aligned with Common Core State Standards for educators, homeschoolers, and parents! Enjoy!

Text-to-Self – Gerry is smaller than the other giraffes, which makes him sad. Have you ever had a problem that made you feel sad? Make a list of the things you could do to make this problem better.

Text-to-Text
* Have you read any books or watched any movies that...

1. Feature a giraffe in them? What are the titles of these books or movies?
2. Show another person overcoming a problem? What is the problem and how does he/she overcome it?
3. Take place in another country? Where?

* Penelope in *'Penelope the Purple Pirate'* (another story by Melissa Northway) is friends with sea animals whose challenges make them different from the other sea animals. Do you think she would have been friends with Gerry? Why?

Text-to-World: The world would be a better place if we did not criticize people who are different. The other giraffes laughed at Gerry because he was not very tall. How could you be a better person and help someone who is different?

Author's Purpose: What lesson do you believe the author is trying to teach you in this story? Why is it important?

Inference: If giraffes spend about half of their day foraging (look for food), what do you suppose they spend the remainder of their day doing?

Cause/Effect: Giraffes have excellent vision. What is the result of their ability to see long distances?

Visualizing: Imagine a world where everyone tried their best to be better at everything that they do. How might our world be better?

Questioning: Africa is the second-largest of the Earth's seven continents. Which continent is the largest?

Determining Importance: Which do you believe is more important: trying your best or always winning? Why?

Predicting: Gerry discovers that practicing improved his ability to play volleyball. How will his skill of practicing help him improve in other areas of his life?

Synthesizing: Using the first person point of view from the voice of Gerry, write the lyrics to a song. Put the words of this song to a familiar tune, such as "Twinkle, Twinkle, Little Star." What would Gerry sing about? Volleyball? His parents? Africa? His friends?

Venn Diagram: The United States and the countries of Africa are different, but they have similarities also. Draw a Venn diagram, label the left circle "The United States," and label the right circle "Africa." List the two countries' similarities in the middle. Make a list explaining how the United States is different on the left side, and list how Africa is different on the right side.

Illustrating : Since each giraffe has its own unique pattern, draw and color a giraffe that is different from any giraffe you have ever seen.

Moral: A moral to a story is a short sentence that is something important you can learn from the story. What lesson did you learn from reading this book?

Summarize: Can you retell the story in three sentences?

Common Core Standards:
RL.1, RL.2, RL.7, RL.9, RIT.1, RIT.2, RIT.9, W.7, W.8, SL.1, SL.2, L.3.

Bloom's Taxonomy:

Remembering: list, describe, write, label, and draw.
Understanding: predict, summarize, and visualize.
Applying: show, illustrate, and choose.
Analyzing: compare, contrast, identify, and explain.
Evaluating: select, choose.
Creating: compose, predict, and design.

This Smarty Activity is the intellectual property of Cyndie Sebourn and Sascyn Publishing, Inc

You may contact me at Cyndie@sascynpublishing.com.
Website: Sascynpublishing.com.

Melissa

Melissa has been writing and creating since she was a youngster. After college, she went on her own adventure to Japan to teach English as a Second Language. During her three years in Japan, she traveled throughout Vietnam and Thailand, which has inspired her writing. Her daughter, a little tomboy, was the inspiration to write a story about overcoming obstacles and always doing your best. She has her Masters in Nutrition and plans to write nutrition books for children. Melissa thanks her husband Lou, the Society of Children's Book Writers and Illustrators, the Children's Book Insider, and her family and friends for their support. Melissa is grateful to her writers' group, editors and illustrators for helping her along the way.

Visit Melissa at: www.melissanorthway.com and at www.dandelionmoms.com

Jennifer

Jennifer Mercede is a professional painter living in Portland, Oregon. Her spontaneous, colorful art has been featured on OPB's Oregon Artbeat, and reproductions are sold through the Land of Nod and Oopsy Daisy catalogues. In 2011, she and fellow Portland artist Chris Haberman, were voted the My Soiree National Artists Champions in Las Vegas. She enjoys sharing her free-spirited techniques in workshops for both adults and children. Jennifer loves to doodle and draw and is happy to have had the opportunity to draw Gerry the Giraffe.

She thanks Melissa Northway for her patience, and her loving family, friends, and fans for their support.

Visit Jennifer's website: www.jennifermercede.com

Made in the USA
San Bernardino, CA
13 December 2013